THE ESSENTIAL BOOK

DISCOVERING MACHU PICCHU

THE INCA TRAIL AND CHOQUEQUIRAU

TEXT AND PHOTOS:

JOSÉ MIGUEL HELFER ARGUEDAS

EDICIONES DEL HIPOCAMPO S.A.C.

THE ESSENTIAL BOOK

DISCOVERING
MACHU PICCHU
THE INCA TRAIL AND CHOQUEQUIRAU

1ST. EDITION, JULY 2004

TEXT AND PHOTOS:

José Miguel Helfer Arguedas

AUTHORS AND EDITORS:

© 2004 Aneta Dukszto and José Miguel Helfer Arguedas

TRANSLATION:

Patricia Cockburn Ruiz

ENGLISH LANGUAGE ADVISER:

Suzanne Finnigan and Katharine Jackson

GRAPHIC DESIGN:

Mario Quiroz Martinez

ILLUSTRATIONS:

Leontina Monzón Brañes

CARTOGRAPHY:

Grupo Geo Graphos S.R.L.

PRE-PRESS:

CECOSAMI S.A.

PRINTING:

Quebecor World Perú S.A.

Legal Deposit Made: 1501032004-4578

ISBN: 9972-894-15-0

EDICIONES DEL HIPOCAMPO S.A.C.

Av. Luis Aldana 227, Urb. Sta. Catalina – Lima 13

Telefax (51-1) 476 2856 – Email: editor@hipocampo.com.pe

Edition: 7,000 copies

www.hipocampo.com.pe

PRINTED IN PERU

THE LOST CITY

THE LOST CITY

MAP OF THE CITY

THE LOST CITY

Machu Picchu was one of the most beautiful sacred cities established by the Incas on top of the mountains bordering the jungle, northeast of Cusco, that housed a chosen lineage of the theocratic Inca nobility.

Machu Picchu is geographically located in the department or region of Cusco, at 2350 masl and at a southern latitude of 13°09'23" and a western longitude of 72°32'34," north of the Vilcabamba Mountain Range over the canyon formed by the Urubamba River.

The Urubamba River or celestial river, as the Incas also called it, was supposed to be the mirror of the Milky Way in Andean cosmology. Several religious complexes were established along its course, for example those of the Sacred Valley, Machu Picchu and others. For the Incas, religion, military power and political power were closely related.

The Spanish conquest stopped the development of the Inca State and destroyed most of the Inca religious, political and administrative centers. There were two motivating factors. Firstly, the desperate search for gold. And secondly, to consolidate the conquest of the new continent for the Spanish Crown.

Nevertheless, Machu Picchu was saved from Iberian barbarism for reasons yet unknown. It was kept safe from the Hispanic conquistadors for several centuries, covered by the green wrap of the neighboring Cusco jungle. This was the situation until 1911, when the North Ame-

THE INCA SPLENDOR

Huascar.

Atahualpa.

Francisco Pizarro, Conqueror of Peru.

THE SPLENDOR OF THE INCAS

The years of splendor of the Incas were no more than one hundred years. The Cusco ethnic group from which the Incas originated, expanded and conquered a great number of regional states that populated the territories of South America. At their finest moment, the Incas extended their frontiers to the south, down to the Maule River (Chile) and to the north, crossing the banks of the Ancasmayo River (Colombia). Their Western and Eastern borders were naturally outlined by the Pacific Ocean and the Amazon Basin, respectively. All this territory that formed the Inca State (some prefer to call it Empire) was called Tahuantinsuyu.

Before the Incas, other local and regional states existed in what is today Peru. Some of these states reached high degrees of cultural, administrative and artistic development, for example Chavin, Paracas, Nasca, Mochica. The Wari culture also expanded to a great extent during the VII and X centuries to almost all the territory that forms Peru today.

Bronze piece representing an adult Inca.

White ceramic Inca bottle found in Cajamarca.

rican explorer Hiram Bingham arrived at the citadel, aided by local peasants. He was searching for the last Inca bastion against the Spaniards; Vilcabamba. Without realizing, he found the lost city of Machu Picchu.

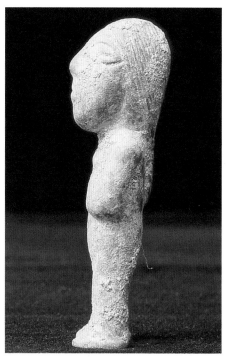

Inca representation of a feminine figure in bronze.

The origins of the Incas go back to the XIII century, when according to legend a foreign ethnic group came from the high plateau region of Lake Titicaca to Cusco, then called Acamama. The local inhabitants of Cusco belonged to the Ayarmaca ethnic group. These foreigners were led by the mythical Manco Capac, who was able to come face to face with the locals and impose his power in the zone.

THE INCA SPLENDOR

Inca Quipu. Demonstrating the high level the Incas reached to control and administrate the accounts of their state through the use of this system of knots and cords that registered information.

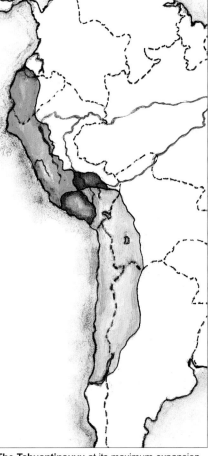

The Tahuantinsuyu at its maximum expansion

Conflict resulted among them which went on for many years, until the final battle in which the chief of the Ayarmaca (Tocay Capac) was captured and this ethnic group was annihilated. The Incas confronted an ethnic group from Andahuaylas, the hardened Chancas, whom they defeated. This, put an end to the first stage of the establishment of their state. This took place around 1498, under the control of Inca Pachacutec.

The second stage began within the same year and is known as the days of Inca splendor and glory. Inca Pachacutec began expanding his domain through military and diplomatic ways.

Reciprocal agreements were used with his neighbors and with more distant states. The success of those agreements was based on the introduction of an economic system, equal for everybody, covering agricultural production, redistribution of crops, religion and administration. This system relied on the theocratic hierarchy of the Inca ruler and his Cusco elite. The nobility of the conquered states who, in many cases, were allowed to keep on

Chimu-Inca Bottle. After the conquest of the Chimor or Chimu by the Incas, the conquered standardized their stylistic patterns according to the Inca norms.

administering their kingdoms, were included in this hierarchy.

The construction of thousands of kilometers of roads was vital for the expansion of the Inca state. This allowed perfect communication among each and every community within the state. The unification of worship of the sun, water and earth as religious axes, was also important, as well as the enforcement of Quechua as the official language.

Tahuantinsuyu was divided into four parts, or "suyu", communicating with Cusco through an extensive road network that began at the sacred center of the Inca capital. Northwest of Cusco, was Chinchaysuyu, Contisuyu to the southwest, Antisuyu to the northeast and Collasuyu to the southeast. This division allowed for better political administration and military control of the state and it probably took into account the geopolitical criteria at the time of the Inca expansion. The Inca state started to decline with the war for the throne between the brothers Huascar and Atahualpa between the years 1524 and 1532. Huascar and Atahualpa were sons of the late Inca Huayna Capac. This Inca died suddenly, as a result of the influenza virus that had arrived at the American continent from Europe,

with the first conquistadores. The second factor that was decisive for the decline of the Incas was the number of new illnesses coming from Europe. These illnesses annihilated the local population and caused great commotion among the Indians, who assumed that these maladies were plagues sent by their gods as punishment. And the coup de grâce came in the form of a group of conquistadores led by Francisco Pizarro. The conquistadores imprisoned Atahualpa (the winner of the war between the Inca brothers) and fatally wounded the Inca State on November 16, 1532.

After the execution of the Inca ruler, in 1533 the different local states cut their ties with Cusco and some of them even joined the Spaniards in their march towards the Inca Capital.

Cusco had not recovered from the destruction caused by Atahualpa's troops in the war against his brother Huascar, when the Hispanic conquistadores and their native allies surrounded Cusco. The city organized the resistance under Manco Inca, who had named himself ruler. He could not resist the Spanish attack for long and retreated with his troops to

Hiram Bingham was born in Honolulu in 1875. He was educated in Yale, California and Harvard and was professor at Harvard and Princeton, even though he made his teaching career in Yale. His political career in the United States took him to become Governor of Connecticut and finally senator for his country. He died in 1956.

Vilcabamba (Northeast of Cusco) where he established the last Inca capital. Manco Inca died in 1542, and three rulers succeeded him, the last one being Tupac Amaru, who was defeated and assassinated by the Spanish troops of Viceroy Toledo in 1572, the year in which the Spanish conquest was consolidated.

THE DISCOVERY

Hiram Bingham, explorer and South American History professor, was born in Honolulu, United States. He wanted to deepen his knowledge about Simon Bolivar's liberating campaign and for this purpose he traveled to Venezuela and Colombia, following the path taken by the Liberator. Afterwards, at the end of 1908, he attended a congress in Santiago de Chile as Official Delegate of the United States, with the intention of continuing with his travels in South America. It was precisely because he

Road covered with vegetation leading to the Putucusi Mountain, facing Machu Picchu. Bingham's exploratory trip must have included enormous difficulties to overcome.

Tarawasi architectural complex visited by Bingham when traveling from Cusco to Abancay. The beautiful archaeological ruins he was coming across along the way, started arousing in him a growing interest in the Incas.

was carrying these credentials that the local authorities gave him all the necessary facilities to travel across the old colonial roads that used to join Buenos Aires and Lima through the Andes.

February 1909, Bingham traveled through the Peruvian mountain region during the month of the heaviest rain of the rainy season, making his trip more difficult. Bingham was already interested in the Incas, a subject about which as he himself recognized, he knew very little. After a long trip, he arrived at the Choquequirau ruins, which, as it was believed at the time, were supposed to contain countless treasures buried by the Incas.

Once back home and teaching at Yale University, Bingham received a proposal to collaborate in an expedition to determine whether the snow capped mountain Coropuna (Arequipa), was the highest one in South America. There were doubts about the Aconcagua being the highest. Some of his colleagues offered him finance to take care of the expenses of a geologist, a naturalist, a doctor, a topographer, an engineer and even a voluntary assistant. Bingham's idea and that of the Yale Peruvian Expedition of 1911, was to travel along the Urubamba River and its surroundings to find the last capital of the Incas, then arrive at the Pacific coast through Arequipa in such a way as to also

be able to climb the Coropuna snow capped mountain.

Bingham studied Colonial documents and a series of writings from the time of the conquest, with the intention of knowing exactly where to go. Those of the Augustinian Father Calancha, were of special interest. He had heard of talk in Cusco about a mysterious lost city, protected by jungle vegetation, at which some peasants and treasure hunters had arrived and which they called Machu Picchu. However, nobody in Cusco believed this information since they thought the last Inca capital was Choquequirau and knew nothing about any ruins further than Ollantaytambo, with neither of these being in the Vilcabamba Valley.

Bingham valued the information of the historian Carlos Romero, who thought that the last Inca capital, Vitcos, was "close to a big white rock next to a water fountain". He was guided by the maps made by the Italian scholar and explorer Antonio Raimondi. Raimondi never found Vitcos, even though he traveled several times to the Vilcabamba Mountain Range (in fact he traveled all over Peru). He only found the small village of Vilcabamba, founded by the first Spanish conquistadors that extracted gold in the area.

Thanks to the economic support of the Italian trader Cesar Lomellini, Bingham was able to organize his expedition, which left Cusco at the beginning of July, 1911.

First they went to the Urubamba Valley and there, the expedition was thrilled with the Ollantaytambo town as well as the Inca fortress. Since 1895, this place had been able to be reached by a rough road.

The expedition traveled through a number of small villages heading northeast, following the course of the Urubamba River, and arriving at Q'ente. Here they noticed a series of ruined constructions on the other side of the river. Bingham sent his topographer across the river to investigate a little further up the left bank. He came back three days later with information about ruins and towns found. The Patallacta Inca complex being the most important of these. The entire site would be inspected later by Bingham and his expedition.

Bingham continued his trip along the bank of the Urubamba and arrived at the Torontoy and Salapunco ruins. He was amazed at the fine finish of some of the buildings and the impressive landscape of the start of the canyon of the Urubamba River.

By July 23, the expedition had reached the Mandor Pampa zone, adjacent to Machu Picchu. Once there, they were received by a suspicious local peasant, Melchor Arteaga, who had a hut that served as a bar and lodgings to travelers. The expedition members decided to camp nearby and not use Arteaga's lodgings.

THE DISCOVERY

The route taken by Bingham to reach Machu Picchu was in most part the same the train joining Aguas Calientes with Cusco, along the Urubamba River, travels today. Some local peasant houses can be seen next to the Inca ruins.

This made the peasant suspicious, Bingham recounts. Fortunately, the expedition included a Cusco policeman, Sergeant Carrasco, who spoke very good Quechua and served as an interpreter. The presence of the policeman calmed the peasant who, after a long conversation, behaved more amiably with the foreigners. When he learnt that the foreigners were looking for ruins that three centuries before could have been the last Inca capital, he cooperated with them and offered important information. He told the expedition that just across the camp were the Huayna Picchu and Machu Picchu mountains, which both had important stone buildings on top, the second one more than the first one.

The following morning, July 24, 1911, was cold and there was a thick layer of fog. Artega, according to Bingham, did not seem to have awoken with the desire of coming out of his hut, in spite of the fact that Bingham had asked him to guide them up the mountains he had described the night before. Never-theless, after offering him one sol as payment, he agreed to do it (according to Bingham himself, that was three or four times more than the usual amount paid per day in those places).

Getting ready to leave, Arteaga was asked about the place where they would be going, and he indicated the top

Small bronze Inca llama.

of the mountain. Seeing this, Binghams colleagues got discouraged and making several excuses, refused to accompany him. So, Bingham climbed alone with Arteaga and Sergeant Carrasco, leaving at ten in the morning that day. They walked for about 45 minutes when Arteaga lead the group to a narrow section of the river. Some sticks of irregular sizes tied up in a very unsafe way, were supposed to serve as a bridge. The fear of falling into the river rapids made Bingham get down on his knees and cross the bridge crawling at a pace of six inches at a time. Once they had reached the other side, they entered into the thick vegetation of the jungle and started the difficult task of climbing for one hour and twenty minutes, at times crawling and holding themselves by only their nails.

After midday, they reached a height of about 600 meters above the river, where they found a hut and some peasants who were pleasantly surprised to see them. They were offered fresh water to drink and some recently cooked potatoes to kill their hunger. These peasants named Richarte and Alvarez (surnames), had recently settled in the Machu Picchu Inca terraces to work them agriculturally, fleeing from tax collectors and military levy.

The zone where Machu Picchu is located had been isolated because of the thick vegetation and lack of access roads. However during the years that Bingham explored the area, the government was building roads to allow for the repopulation of the area and that meant the arrival of peasants who cut and burnt the vegetation to obtain agricultural land.

Because the distance to be covered to reach the top was not large, having rested, Bingham decided to keep climbing. The peasant Arteaga decided to stay down talking to the other peasants and sent a boy instead as guide. Sergeant Carrasco kept on climbing with Bingham, more out of curiosity than because it was his duty, as Bingham relates. The North American explorer began to notice more imposing terraces of enormous size. What surprised him was to suddenly find a series of finely finished Inca walls, covered by the vegetation of centuries but visible to the eye. Suddenly, the boy took Bingham among bushes and bamboo canes to a carved, polished and well finished cave that must have been, according to Bingham, the Royal Tomb. The explorer was touring Machu Picchu for the first time.

Bingham returned to his country with the news of finding the Machu Picchu Citadel. This find caught the attention of the world and in particular of Yale University and the National Geographic Society. Both institutions

Inca stone mallet head similar to the ones Bingham found in Machu Picchu.

decided to back Bingham to explore and study the ruins. As a result, the Peruvian Expeditions to Machu Picchu in 1912 and 1915, were organized.

As well as Bingham and the local inhabitants, six North American investigators participated in the first expedition. The second expedition had a larger budget and included twenty North American investigators with differing expertise, from topographers, geographers and doctors, to naturalists and anthropologists. In addition there were numerous local peasants working to clear the thick vegetation and dig for tombs and other relics.

Bingham and his crew were very surprised at not finding many tombs in Machu Picchu. The North American explorer indicated that "a careful counting of the skeletons and bones found in the different caves and tombs seems to show the remains of one hundred

Inca pitcher also known as "aribalo". The conic base made it possible to attach it to the floor by inserting it in a small hole.

and seventy three individuals from which maybe one hundred and fifty correspond to women, an extraordinary percentage, unless these were the Women Chosen by the Sun." The rest of the people connected to Machu Picchu, apart from the servants, farmers and soldiers would have been buried outside the city. This would explain, for Bingham, the absence of more remains.

The report also indicated that tracks of previous diggings were found, probably made by Incas before leaving the citadel or maybe by local treasure hunters. Bingham adds that no gold or silver objects were found, but only articles of bronze and other metals, including wood, stone and bones. In all, Bingham mentions 521 ceramic pieces identified, and around 220 metallic objects.

He emphasied a bronze knife with the figure of a fisher boy and his catch, which he described as the most beautiful pre Columbian piece of art in all America, which is found at the museum of Yale University.

It is not clear what Bingham's expeditions exactly took from Peru. Bingham's reports identify some objects (the ones mentioned above) and Yale University indicates that at present they have 4904 pre Columbian objects from Bingham's expeditions. However, according to the official report of the Peruvian government made in 1916, Bingham took 74 boxes full of bone remains, mummies, ceramics, textiles, metallic and wooden objects, with no gold or silver objects being registered.

But there were always doubts about the report given the magnitude of the Inca city and its importance for the nobility. All scholars agree that it was impossible not to have found objects made with precious metals in Machu Picchu. This lost city of the Incas was kept safe from Spanish depredation for four hundred years and could not have been the exception and not held beautiful ceremonial and liturgical pieces as well as royal ornaments made of gold or silver.

Bingham was a personal friend of the then Peruvian president, Augusto Leguia. This allowed him to easily obtain authorization to take out of the country the archaeological pieces mentioned on a temporary loan basis and for study purposes. At present, the Peruvian government is having conversations with Yale University to return the pieces and start an archaeological museum in Machu Picchu.

THE CITADEL

The names by which the different places of the citadel are identified are arbitrary and correspond to the suppositions of Bingham and the other investigators of the complex. Due to a lack of evidence of what the city really was, the investigators tried to explain the purpose of each building of the archaeological complex.

Machu Picchu has been divided into two ample sectors or zones: agricultural and urban. The agricultural zone is located at the south and is formed by numerous ample terraces. Not all the terraces were agricultural and probably served as supports for the structures of other terraces and constructions. They facilitated access to the steep zones of the mountain and had the aesthetic purpose of harmonizing with the architecture of the complex. The terraces had small steps fixed to the walls, so it was possible to shift easily from one terrace to the other.

The urban zone is surrounded by a big wall and is separated from the agricultural zone by a big stairway that runs from top to bottom parallel to a dry moat. The urban sector has a main entrance gate and consists of numerous and varied buildings, from simple rooms to beautiful temples, with many water fountains and channels, squares, pyramids and hundreds of stairways.

Orchid Lycaste locusta.

General view of the Machu Picchu citadel, from the Putucusi mountain, on the other side of the Urubamba River. The photo clearly shows the division of the agricultural and urban sectors of the city, as well as part of the present access road to the ruins.

THE CITADEL

AGRICULTURAL SECTOR

The agricultural zone is located south of the complex and is formed by terraces on both sides of the mountain, the eastern (facing the Putucusi mountain) as well as on the western side. The road connecting the citadel with the Inti Punku (Sun Gate) and with the Inca trail arrives from the east. An important number of tombs were found on this side, which is why it is called the Upper Cemetery. It is there, at the Upper Cemetery where an enormous stone block with some engraved shapes, called the Funerary Rock, rests.

This rock has been engraved and polished in such a way that it looks like an operating table. It was most likely used to embalm the bodies of priests and other important people, or maybe to perform some type of ritual or sacrifice of animals or humans.

Finally, crowning a spectacular view

Funerary Rock located in the upper cemetery of the complex.

Terraces on the east side of the agricultural sector. The Caretaker's hut can be seen at the top, and further up, the Machu Picchu mountain summit.

The Caretaker's hut crowns a spectacular view of Machu Picchu. Shown at sunset.

of the citadel, there is a small construction from which it is possible to watch the access points to the city from the South. This place is called the Caretaker's hut, which was probably its purpose.

At the same eastern side of the agricultural sector and by the present visitor entrance, there is a series of five buildings, one at each level of the terraces. Bingham called these buildings, Guardian Houses, as they seem to control one of the most important points of access to the city.

Machu Picchu seen from Inti Punku. Part of the Inca Trail leading to Machu Picchu can be observed in the foreground. A little further is the agricultural zone and its impressive and numerous terraces.

AGRICULTURAL SECTOR

Drawbridge, on the western side.

Masdevallia veitchiana orchid photographed in the zone.

Inca jar.

On the western side of the agricultural zone, on the highest point of the complex, there is a long building with ten entrances or doorways, eight at the front and one at each side. The building

AGRICULTURAL SECTOR

Guardian Houses.

is one story and the back wall rests on the mountain. It gives the impression, because of the magnitude of the construction, that it was used as military barracks. However, some researchers reject this idea since the very wide doors do not allow for heat to be contained in a very cold area. They maintain that it was a kind of workshop for the production of textiles or other types of objects used in worshiping. It is known as the Building of the Ten Doors.

There is a road towards the south of this sector that follows the sinuosity of the mountain. It is interrupted at the edge of the cliff and the breach has been joined with trunks resting on a stone against the mountain. This was definitely one of the best controlled accesses to the city, and this mechanism of trunks that served as a bridge is called the Drawbridge.

Building of the Ten Doors.

INTI PUNKU

Panoramic view of the Machu Picchu complex from the road leading to Inti Punku (Sun Gate). The Putucusi Mountain can be seen at the right, surrounded by the Urubamba River and the road from the town of Aguas Calientes. The road on the left through which visitors arrive, goes up zigzagging at the left. The mountain on the left is the Huayna Picchu (Huayna means young and Picchu peak, while Machu means old).

This construction is found at the Inti Punku road facing the Urubamba River canyon and appears to be a small ritual or ceremonial complex. The large polished rock on the right most likely served to make offerings to the mountains (Apus), while the rooms with small niches probably housed the priests in charge of the rituals.

Enclosed space at Inti Punku. The distance between Machu Picchu and this place is approximately one kilometer and it is located at 2650 masl.

URBAN SECTOR

The eastern urban sector (in the photo) is separated from the western one by a large esplanade.

The urban zone is formed by the city itself. It begins at a moat or trench that separates it from the agricultural area. It consists of a series of enclosed spaces which have different levels of perfection with regard to the stone work. Some buildings were finished with polished stones fitting perfectly together, while others were finished with small stones of irregular dimensions joined with mud mortar and have an external finishing.

Beautiful example of a trapezoidal Inca window. The base of the wall shows polished stone blocks that are larger than the ones on top. The top part is not as well finished. It could have been covered with mud and then painted over.

The characteristics of the Inca architecture are the use of trapezoidal windows and niches and of stone spikes that served to hold the roofs.

The perfection of the stone work is closely related to the purpose of the room and the importance of those who inhabited or made use of it. The most beautiful building is a tower, very similar to the one of Koricancha in Cusco, which Bingham interpreted as a temple consecrated to the maximum Inca deity: the Sun.

The urban zone consists of a western and eastern sector divided by a great square. The buildings located west were the ones mainly consecrated to liturgy. However, it must be taken into account that there is little information about this city. Much of the data handled consists mostly of speculations and suppositions by diverse scholars, with Bingham, being the most important source of information.

Dry moat dividing the agricultural and the urban sectors. It runs parallel to the wall protecting the city from top to bottom.

In spite of this, it is possible to analyze the architectural characteristics of the city and its buildings, which undoubtedly will help us to understand a little bit of the hidden mysteries of this magical lost city.

The buildings are mainly rectangular with trapezoidal doorways and niches, and walls that are slightly bent towards the inside of the buildings.

These characteristics repeat themselves in Cusco and in many other places reached by the Incas.

The rooms are mostly one or two levels, and the floor of the top level is made of wood. The roof had a structure of trunks over which they placed dried, rain resistant straw (ichu) and this structure was attached to the walls through supporting stone spikes.

Water, a symbol of fertility, was a sacred element for the Incas. Because of this, sixteen water fountains and diverse subterranean and open channels were built to transport it through the city.

Definitely, water worshiping was constantly present in the activities of the Incas at Machu Picchu.

Communication inside the city was through passages, roads and hundreds of stairways going up and down the

URBAN SECTOR

Entrance to Machu Picchu urban sector.

different levels. Because the city was built at different levels, the inhabitants moved around the city as if moving from one terrace to the next. This incomplete-pyramidal structure is characteristic of the Inca religious architecture, which leads to the belief that Machu Picchu was in fact a city dedicated to liturgy that housed a select group of noblemen and priests consecrated to worshiping the sun, water and mother earth.

This kind of construction is commonly found in Inca architecture, with three walls only, one very tall as if made to support a second level. The use of stone spikes to serve as supports for the roof can also be seen.

Urban sector
Entrance Gate, next
to the dry moat.

Inside the urban sector Entrance Gate. Notice the security mechanisms, made of stone, to place a pole at the entrance. The ring at the top served to raise the pole while there was an adjustment system at each side. The wall shows two types of finishing, the top part is simpler, with smaller stones joined together with mud mortar, while the lower part from the floor to the threshold, has been built with homogenous, polished and well-fitted blocks.

Passage that connects a line of buildings at the upper complex. Note that these were two-story constructions and had a mechanism to support the roof, made with tree trunks and dried straw. The terraces of the agricultural sector and the Caretaker's hut can be appreciated in the background. The peak of the Machu Picchu Mountain can also be seen.

UPPER COMPLEX OF BUILDINGS

The group of buildings located at one side of the Entrance Gate to the city are known as the Upper Complex of Buildings. They were constructed in rows which follow the contours of the mountain. The passages that connect the buildings with each other are straight and extend from north to south, while the façades and windows of the rooms face east. The west walls of these buildings served as supports.

These rooms were probably used for housing, even when some buildings have two floors or levels. According to some scholars, the second level must have served as storage for grain or other foodstuffs.

Machu Picchu urban sector.

URBAN SECTOR

This photo shows the way in which the Incas employed the natural shape of the mountains to help support their constructions.

The windows of these buildings look to the Urubamba River canyon and to the Putucusi mountain. Huayna Picchu rises at the back.

General view of the Upper Complex of Buildings.

General view of Machu Picchu with the quarry in front.

QUARRIES

The quality of the stone work achieved by the Incas in such a short time is surprising. The period between the time the Incas were at their best until the Spanish conquistadors arrived was less than one hundred years. The Incas inherited certain art and architectural characteristics from previous cultures. For example the Tiahuanaco (or Tiwanaku) culture, that developed a notable religious and mythical architecture. There are other monumental buildings in Peru, with that of the Chavin culture (a thousand years before Christ) being one of the best.

Cusco is the Inca architectural jewel, specially when it comes to the fine stone work. Koricancha is the most beautiful and well made, but there are other impressive cyclopean monuments like Sacsayhuaman, Ollantaytambo (Cusco) and Vilcashuaman (Ayacucho), amongst others. The characteristics of fine stone work and the use of very large stone blocks in constructions are also found in Machu Picchu. However, it should be mentioned that the Incas, especially in the Andes (it should be noted that constructions on the

Stone blocks in the Machu Picchu quarry. It can be seen that one of the blocks was abandoned in the midst of the cutting process.

coast were made of adobe) used stone as a mechanism of identification with the land, as Investigator Rebecca Stone-Miller

indicated in her book "Art of the Andes". The investigator maintains that "the Incas had a special feeling of

Stone block that happened to be in the mountain, used by the Incas as support for a room. It can be seen that underneath the block, the Incas built a base of cobblestones. On the right, going up the stairs, there are other rocks the Inca architects took advantage of.

transformation with the stones, which they thought to be alive and could be changed into people and vice versa." This identity motivated them to manipulate the stones and the mountains with a sense of expression in accordance with the purposes of the State.

The Incas extracted their raw material from quarries close to their constructions and transported the big blocks employing a lot of people. They also scattered small stones on the way, which served as transporting wheels on which to slide the big blocks.

The quarry that provided the stone material in Machu Picchu was close by, next to the Sacred Plaza, and stones that were abandoned in the midst of the cutting process can still be seen. What is amazing until this day is the perfect carving of the stones that made them fit perfectly with each other without the need for any adhering material and without leaving any space between them, just like a mosaic.

The less important constructions were built with small cobblestones joined together with mud mortar and smaller stones that served as wedges. For palaces and religious buildings, they used bigger blocks, very well polished and fitting perfectly. To support terraces in monumental constructions they used gigantic stone blocks, as can be seen in Sacsayhuaman or in Machu Picchu itself.

Numerous stone blocks at the Machu Picchu quarry.

Main Ceremonial Fountain in Machu Picchu.

Ceremonial Center, with the circular tower of the Temple of the Sun next to it. The water fountains flow between both stairways. There are sixteen water fountains in Machu Picchu. According to the Peruvian scholar, Federico Kauffmann Doig, the purpose of Machu Picchu was to administer the agricultural production of the area but also to "be used as a sanctuary for water or magical pluvial propitiatory rites."

This fountain lets out only a trickle of water, controlled by the authorities of the complex. If they let the water flow normally it would be a lot bigger; water is fed through subterranean channels.

Inside part of the Ceremonial Fountain. The scholars believe that ceremonies to worship water took place here.

CEREMONIAL CENTER

The zone where this three-walled construction is located (the Incas called this type of enclosed space "huayrana") is known as the Group of the Sun. This is because the Ceremonial Center, the Liturgical or Ceremonial Fountains and the Temple of the Sun with the Royal Tomb underneath it, is located there. In addition what supposedly was the Princess or Ñusta Palace is next to it.

Investigators specializing in the Incas agree that this "huayrana", looking toward the east of the citadel, was the place where the rites and worshiping of water took place. In an agricultural culture like that of the Incas, this was vital for the preservation of society.

Water represented fertility and therefore, life. But in the religious-magical sense, this worship was associated not only with nature, but with the beliefs and myths that formed part of Inca cosmology. As indicated before, the Urubamba River was considered as the mirror image of the Milky Way and as a result, it was a celestial river. The Incas channeled the natural water fountains and created their own fountains. This enabled them to worship the water that flowed through the path made by them from the top, which joined the celestial river down the bottom of the canyon.

When the Spaniards arrived, the chroniclers of the conquest were surprised at the cleanliness and tidiness of the Inca noblemen and the baths they took

everyday, with special attendants for that purpose. It is true that there is no palace, administrative center or Inca complex without ceremonial water fountains.

Inca religion is quite complex. It did not have the one and only god not even the hierarchy of gods that are mistakenly attributed to it. For the Incas there were three superposed universes: the world of the living, the world of the dead and the world of the gods. In the world of the living there existed a hierarchy of priests and Inca nobility, where the supreme leader, the Inca, had divine powers. For this reason, his subjects could not look him in the face or talk to him, except through the priests acting as intermediaries. The world of the dead was like the extension of this world where one had to arrive

Ceremonial Center.

carrying one's possessions and powers to reproduce the same conditions of existence. That is the reason why they were mummified, and the body and properties were taken care of as if the person was still alive. Dead Incas had influence over the power of the State through their families and servants, a system that was called "panaca".

There is a lot of controversy and misinterpretation regarding the world of the gods and the number of gods the Incas had. The more serious scholars agree that this distortion originated from the fact that when the Incas expanded, they assimilated the local idols of the conquered states. In the end they all agree in the worship of the three basic elements, Sun, water and earth. There are variations in the names given and the other elements build on the three basic elements.

Beautiful Inca ceramic piece representing a water pitcher over the head or a plough piece. The relationship with fertility is evident.

Lightning, for example, is a variation of water that means fertility. The mountains (Apus) were also related to water. It is important to note that the chain of life reproduces with the joining of the basic three elements. Some scholars go even further maintaining that the Inca religion had only two basic worship elements: water and earth. The sun, for them, was identified with water.

The "pachamama" or mother earth, was represented by a symbol of a set of steps, which is found everywhere in Inca complexes, for example in the Intihuatana or on Funerary Rock in Machu Picchu.

In short, the Inca religion as all other Andean religions of three thousand years ago, based their beliefs on rites that ensured the survival of their agricultural societies, employing magic and religious worship as well as the knowledge to achieve fertility and abundance of the land. To achieve this, the Incas did not stop at worshiping water or making payments to the land, they also made various types of sacrifices with animals and human beings. And Machu Picchu definitely fits in as a settlement specially designed for the religious activities of worshiping the sun, water and mother earth.

Photo next page: The Temple of the Sun in the foreground and in the back the Putucusi mountain surrounded by the Urubamba River.

Temple of the Sun and underneath, the grotto that forms the Royal Tomb.

TEMPLE OF THE SUN

When Bingham found this finely finished, semicircular tower, he immediately thought that since its shape was similar to that of the Koricancha Temple of the Sun in Cusco, this must have been also a temple dedicated to worshiping the sun. And apparently he was not wrong. Two of the windows of this tower are aligned according to the points where the sun rises on the summer and winter solstices, the longest and the shortest day of the year, respectively. Based on the solstices, the Inca astronomers could give information regarding the sowing and harvesting seasons and could recognize seasonal changes, when to sow certain products. The observation of the sun was complemented with the observation of the sky during the night to learn about the constellations and their appearances and

Window of the Serpents, next to the Ceremonial Center.

Rectilinear back and lateral north walls of the Temple of the Sun. The characteristic internal bending of Inca walls can be appreciated.

Beautiful niches on the inside wall of the Temple of the Sun.

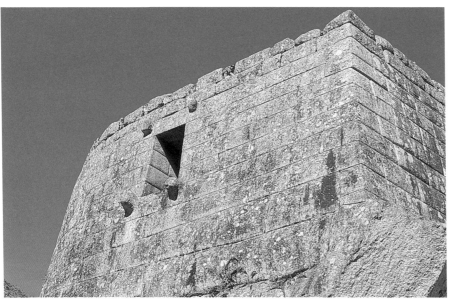

Window looking east. The first sunrays illuminate it directly during the winter solstice.

Beautiful entrance door to the Temple of the Sun. As it can be observed, the entrance was controlled by a security mechanism indicating the importance of these buildings.

disappearances. This also gave them useful information for agricultural purposes. The outside windows on the Temple of the Sun present some cylindrical protrusions whose purpose is unknown. There are speculations as to whether they could have served as supports for some kind of external gadget or decoration related to the solstice rites or had some meaning just as they are.

Southern side of the semicircular Temple of the Sun.

The Temple of the Sun has been built over a huge, finely polished rock, with the walls being built following the natural contour of the original rock. There is a grotto under the temple called the Royal Tomb, where some tombs were found.

The wall next to the Ceremonial Center (northern side) has a large trapezoidal window with some holes in its lower part. Up to now, nobody knows what the purpose for those holes was. Some maintain that they served to hold something that hung from the window, and others believe they were used to introduce serpents to the temple during some particular ceremonies. That is why it is called the Window of the Serpents.

The room is also beautifully finished on the inside, with perfectly fitting stone blocks and a series of the typical niches of Inca architecture. The priests must have used them to place their liturgical ornaments in.

Today, the Temple of the Sun can be reached from the northern side, but originally there was a wall blocking all

Note the protrusions around the window.

access. This wall was removed to improve the circulation of visitors. The Incas had designed only one entrance to the temple which the Ñusta Palace shared. This door is the most beautiful in all of Machu Picchu and has the typical security mechanism of Inca architecture, that is, a ring on top and two small built-in stone cylinders at both sides of the door.

The building on the left is the Ñusta Palace. The peak of the Huayna Picchu Mountain emerges behind the tower of the Temple of the Sun.

Interior of the Temple of the Sun tower seen from the Window of the Serpents. The rock of the base has been carved giving it the shape of a table or altar, also with the set of steps symbol (to the right). The entire perimeter wall which is bent inwards, is finely finished. The top rows, as it can be seen, have collapsed due to rain and the passing of time.

Opposite page. Winter solstice in the Temple of the Sun.

Façade of the Ñusta Palace. The stairway to the right leads to the Temple of the Sun.

Internal side of entrance door to the Ñusta Palace.

Great window or door connecting the Ñusta Palace with the Temple of the Sun.

Palace interior. Notice the inclination of the walls and the beautiful trapezoidal niches. This is undoubtedly, an extremely beautiful building.

THE ÑUSTA PALACE

This building is next to the Temple of the Sun; it is two-stories high and is built with blocks fitting perfectly with each other and has a high quality finish. It has a rectangular base with walls sloping inwards and has some stone spikes on the top part of the wall that must have served to hold the roof. The room has a small window on the façade and a bigger one connecting with the Temple of the Sun at the level of the second floor.

It is called the Ñusta Palace in the supposition that it must have served to house an Inca princess or Ñusta, or a priestess specially considered within the Inca nobility. Bingham deducted that this was a very important building since it was in the Group or Quarter of the Sun. It was situated next to the Temple of the Sun, having an exclusive entrance to it and also due to its beautiful finish.

External part of the Royal Tomb.

Some investigators believe that this room was a kind of detention center for virgins who were to be sacrificed to the sun or to water, or who would participate in some religious rite related to these deities.

This is not a preposterous idea if one takes into account the proximity of this building to the tower next to it and the connection between the two through the upper window of the Ñusta Palace. There is also a stone table in the Temple of the Sun that could have well served for said sacrifices.

On the other side, the tower is also connected to the Ceremonial Center and the Main Fountain through the Window of the Serpents. In fact, these three places form part of the ceremonial complex, the Group of the Sun.

ROYAL TOMB

The Royal Tomb is located exactly under the tower of the Temple of the Sun. The Incas sculpted the rock that serves as the base for the temple and built a mausoleum that was the tomb of an important person (thus the name.)

Outside to the right, there is a carved rock with three steps (symbol of the pachamama or mother earth). This rock has been harmoniously joined to the huge rock that holds the Temple of the Sun, with small finely polished cobblestones. This is characteristic of the Inca religious architecture, as can be appreciated from the Moon Temple (in the Huayna Picchu Mountain) and other religious complexes located on the Inca trail and other places in what used to be their vast territory.

On the inside, this carved rock has two wider platform steps that meet a wall. This wall has been constructed in perfect harmony with the entrance. It is cut diagonally running parallel with the roof of the grotto. All this is made out of stone block, polished with great dexterity and of eminently symbolic character.

The inside walls of the cave of the Royal Tomb are covered with perfectly united cobblestones and there are four trapezoidal niches in the walls of the size of a door.

It is also important to observe the cylindrical stone spikes that protrude from the top part of the walls. These may have served to support some funeral gear or tomb ornament, since the space is so small that they could not have served to support the beams of a roof.

Inside the Royal Tomb. Note the fine construction finish, the harmony of its lines and geometric architectural shapes.

In this photo it is possible to appreciate both carved sides of the rock. Bingham found the tomb of an important person in this place, and the characteristic of the burial leads one to believe that it was related to an Inca ruler, probably the highest authority in Machu Picchu. That is why the explorer called the place the Royal Mausoleum.

Inner patio of the Group of the King. The first door to the left leads to what would be the bedroom of the ruler. The door to the right leads to the entrance or exit and next to it there is a small altar to the right. Some engraved rocks can be seen on the floor of the patio.

THE GROUP OF THE KING

Hiram Bingham named the enclosed spaces located facing the stairways of the Ceremonial Center, the Group of the King believing that this is where the highest authority of the city must have resided. Entrance and exit to this area is through the same spot, therefore its security is significant and the architectural finish of the inside buildings is great.

The entrance is through a narrow passage leading to the main patio, but first there is a small hall with high walls where a carved rock with a hollow protrusion in the shape of a ring, can be seen. This rock with the ring shape is called the "hangman's stone" although it has nothing to do with the name. Most probably it was used for some kind of rite.

Detail of the carved stone ring.

Peculiar carved stone called "the hangman's stone" at the entrance of the Group of the King.

Two beautiful trapezoidal doors at the Group of the King, the room and the workroom are separated by the patio.

Beautiful trapezoidal niches of the bedroom.

Side wall of the bedroom.

External section of the buildings of the Group of the King.

In the main patio, to the left hand side, there is a stone platform rising from the floor that leads to a fairly tall wall with two trapezoidal niches. This place was probably used to contain liturgical ornaments or maybe it housed the mummy of some "panaca" of an ancient ruler.

In the patio, facing this stone platform, there is carved rock pointing to the room mentioned. This carved stone has two sections, one in the shape of a triangle on top and a rhomboid one on the base, and next to it there is a smaller, circular one. Both must have formed part of a mini liturgical complex where they were used to hold offerings.

There is a room in front of the patio facing south which Bingham thought could have been the bedroom of the Inca ruler, which has ten trapezoidal niches, as nicely finished as the rest of the building.

At the other side of the patio there is another room, bigger than the previous one, which Bingham considered could have been the office, or place of work of the monarch. This room has twelve beautiful niches.

Interior of the office or place of work of the ruler. The peak of Machu Picchu mountain can be seen in the background.

View of the Sacred Plaza. The quarries are behind it and further up to the south are the agricultural zone and the peak of Machu Picchu Mountain. On both sides is the Urubumba River canyon, that surrounds the city.

THE SACRED PLAZA

It consists of a platform on which the Incas built enclosed spaces of religious character, leading one to believe that a series of rites related to the buildings around it must have taken place in this square. These buildings are, on the east side, The Temple of the Three Windows, to the south, The House of the High Priest, to the north, The Principal Temple and to the west, only the foundations of a semicircular construction called The Temple of the Moon. There is no evidence about it being such a temple, but it seems logical to believe that it was destined to observe the west, where the sun sets, and probably used at night, maybe for rites related to the stars or perhaps the moon.

The basis for this is that on that side, a bit to the south, is where the stars that form the Southern Cross appear. There is a rock on the floor, carved in a rhomboid shape, very close to these semicircular foundations that points to the southwest and when the four points of the rhombus are connected, they form a cross.

Many visitors arrive at Machu Picchu with the idea of participating in the different rites the local shamans carry out on special dates, like this one celebrating the winter solstice at the Sacred Plaza.

Machu Picchu Sacred Plaza. On the left lies the Temple of the Three Windows. In the foreground the House of the High Priest. On the right, the semicircular base of an observatory. In the middle, the back of the Principal Temple can be seen. The Chamber or Room of the Ornaments is in the lower part of the picture, to the right.

Temple of the Three Windows. The Intihuatana pyramid rises at the right.

TEMPLE OF THE THREE WINDOWS

This room is located at the east side of the esplanade or Sacred Plaza. It is an impressive building because of its huge, finely polished stone blocks that fit perfectly one with the other. The room is rectangular and has only three walls, the open side faces the square with a group of blocks in the middle. One of these blocks seems to have served as a column.

The three windows, after which the building is named, are on the opposite side, flanked by two big niches. The lateral walls have a small window each on top and some of the stone spikes used by the Incas to support the roof.

Inside view of the Temple of the Three Windows. Notice the niches at the end of the east wall and the columns on the west side. The blocks on the floor must have formed part of this room. Their original location is not known. Next to the column in the middle, there is a carved stone with the set of steps symbol.

View of the external façade of the Temple of the Three Windows that faces east. This shows how the Sacred Plaza rests on a series of terraces on the slope of the mountain. Note the difference in size of the stones used for the terraces and those of the Temple of the Three Windows.

Left, Sunrise during the winter solstice. The first sunrays come in through the windows. **Right:** A small window on the lateral, northern wall of the temple. The one corresponding to the opposite wall has fallen down as a result of rain and time.

HOUSE OF THE HIGH PRIEST

Bingham called the building located south of the square the House of the High Priest. He thought that the High Priest would come out of it to direct the liturgical acts that used to take place in the square. This building is of a lower architectural quality. It has two doors that lead to the square and a series of niches inside.

Façade of the House of the High Priest or Willaj Uma.

Front view of the House of the High Priest. The peak of Machu Picchu Mountain rises in the background.

Principal Temple. It is one of the buildings with the finest stone polishing finish. It can be seen that the back wall has been severely damaged by nature and is at risk of collapsing.

Notice the size of the stone blocks on the base of the walls of the Principal Temple. The Chamber of the Ornaments is on the left.

Back of the Principal Temple. The damage to the wall structure can be seen. Notice the small finely finished stone wall attached to the mountain.

PRINCIPAL TEMPLE

It is positioned facing the House of the High Priest and of finer architecture that the latter. It has three walls with the empty side next to the square. The stone blocks used in its construction are as big as the ones of the Temple of the Three Windows. The joining and polishing of the stones are finely finished.

There is a small stone altar on the back wall and the three walls have very well finished niches (five on each side and seven on the back). Unfortunately, the structure of the back wall has been affected by some seismic movement and is in danger of collapsing.

This rhomboid carved stone is located at one side the Principal Temple in the Sacred Plaza. Its top vertex points to the Southwest, precisely at the point where the Southern Cross constellation appears. At the edge of the square, next to the west terraces are the semicircular foundations that probably belonged to an observatory to watch the moon and the stars, hence the name Temple of the Moon.

Chamber of the Ornaments. This is the name given by Bingham to this rectangular enclosure located behind the Principal Temple because of its proximity to it. However, Bingham himself admits that this room may have been a funeral chamber, mausoleum or the tomb of some high ranking personage of Inca nobility.

Semicircular foundation of the so-called Temple of the Moon at the Machu Picchu Sacred Plaza.

Intihuatana Pyramid, with the Sacred Plaza in front. To the right and in the background, the two huayranas flanking the Sacred Rock.

This rock imitating the shapes of the mountains in front of Machu Picchu is found at the edge of the road leading to the top of the pyramid, where the Intihuatana is located. The highest peak on the carved rock would correspond to the peak of Huayna Picchu, in the background.

This ring carved on a stone is located at the edge of the road going up to the Intihuatana. Its purpose is not known, but it was definitely not decorative.

Beautiful trapezoidal windows on top of the pyramid.

INTIHUATANA

The Intihuatana is located on top of a pyramid built at the highest point of the urban sector of Machu Picchu. Its name means "where the sun is tied up" and this was precisely its objective. The purpose of the religious rites was to stop the sun from disappearing, or in any case, ensure its return.

For many years, this stone was considered a solar timepiece, in the belief that the Incas used it to measure time. However, even though this is not correct, it is not entirely wrong. While the rock does not measure time, it can indicate the position of the sun at its solstice and therefore, offer useful information for agriculture with respect to the time to sow and the time to harvest. This information was vital for agricultural communities.

According to Andean cosmology, the climate could be sympathetic to them if

Intihuatana
"where the sun is tied up."

The top of the pyramid where the Intihuatana rests. The frontal esplanade where these beautiful stone walls were built, with well-placed niches to the side, seems to have been the place where the rites related to the sun were prepared.

they worshiped their gods appropriately. Droughts and floods were punishment and they had to sacrifice animals and human beings to calm the divine rage. Astrological observation was quite advanced at the time of the Incas. According to existing chronicles, they were able to anticipate eclipses, were familiar with the phases of the moon, knew the position of the stars and created their own constellations.

Along with this knowledge of the cosmos, the Incas knew they had to pray to the spirit of the mountains, the spirit of water and the sun for the fertility of their land and the appropriateness of the climate. That is why the Intihuatana was used in a rite that was intended to ensure the presence of the Sun on the shortest day of the year (winter solstice). As its name indicates, the sun was tied to this monument with the intention of impeding its disappearance.

Probably, the priests and astronomers joined faith and knowledge in a religious act of the greatest importance for the Inca state.

This was the most important celebration. The shortest day of the year was identified, which in other words meant that during six months of the year the sun started disappearing for a few more minutes each day until it reached the winter solstice.

The Intihuatana before the damage suffered to one of its vertical axes.

Occidental terraces of the Intihuatana pyramid.

This was the day when death turned into life. From the following day, the sun would stay a few more minutes longer each day, being born again and offering more hours of light and warmth, and therefore a favorable stage for agriculture. It is

From the opposite angle, looking from north to south, it is possible to see the back of the Intihuatana. Notice that the right vertex of the vertical axis is slightly mutilated. In 2001, a TV commercial for a local brewery was being filmed there and due to the negligence of some operators, a heavy crane fell on top of the Intihuatana chipping one of the corners of the column. The damage was beyond repair and now the Inca altar looks slightly mutilated.

believed that the Intihuatana was also used during eclipses in similar rites for permanence of the sun.

Federico Kauffmann Doig indicates that there is a Pre-Hispanic myth called Intihuatana relating that "the forebears had the power of tying the sun and they did this in order to make the day longer to be able to cultivate the land for more hours and ensure a better and larger production of food".

Other investigators offer similar theories with respect to the use and meaning of this peculiarly shaped stone, which bears the set of steps symbol representing the "pachamama" or mother earth. Its relationship with the fertility of the soil is clear, as is also the fear the Incas had of natural disasters, specially droughts and excessive rain. In this respect, there is a great deal of evidence that the Incas made human sacrifices to calm the rage of nature and obtain better results from the land.

It should be mentioned that some scholars maintain that the vertical axis of the Intihuatana would be more related to the mountains (Apus) and to fertility symbolized by water rather than to the sun. This theory nevertheless, is refuted by the Pre-Hispanic myths and reports that confirm its relationship with the permanence of the sun.

Orchid Odontoglossum mystacinum.

The entire Pyramid. In the foreground, the main square of Machu Picchu separating the western and eastern urban sector.

Great esplanade or Main Square. This is the biggest of the urban sector. The eastern urban sector rises to the right, the Usnu to the left and the two "huayranas" of the Sacred Rock further to the left. Huayna Picchu is in the background.

SQUARES

The great esplanade between the two elevations of the urban sector that divides it into the eastern and western sides, has basically three levels, forming three squares. The largest one is called the Main Square. This square is located exactly under the Intihuatana pyramid and celebrations must have taken place there with a great number of people. Soldiers, dancers during liturgical rites, or the local population gathered here following the rites that took place at the Intihuatana.

There is a small square in front of the Temple of the Three Windows, which probably served as a place for numerous people to congregate during the ceremonies that took place in this temple or on the Sacred Plaza. It is important to mention that Bingham reported having found innumerable ceramic fragments in this place, in front of the Temple of the Three Windows. As is well known, the Incas used to break their ceramics into pieces, throwing them down during special rites as payment to the land and for fertility.

Square located behind the Prison Group Sector or Temple of the Condor.

Visitors take a rest on the esplanades located in front of the Temple of the Three Windows.

View of the Machu Picchu mountain from the Main Square. To the right is the Temple of the Three Windows. A bit further is the Caretaker's hut crowning the terraces of the agricultural zone and on its right side is the Building of the Ten Doors.

General view of the northern side of Machu Picchu. The two huayranas or three-walled enclosures can be seen flanking the Sacred Rock. In the background is Huayna Picchu.

SACRED ROCK

At the northern end of Machu Picchu, just before the road leading to the top of Huayna Picchu and to the Temple of the Moon, there is a square with two three-wall enclosures. These are built at the northern and southern sides of the square. The Incas called this type of enclosure huayrana.

At the east side of the square, there is a great stone block that has been carved reproducing the shape of the mountains behind the rock. The rock rests on a rectangular pedestal.

Back terraces of the eastern urban sector, next to the Sacred Rock.

For some scholars, this rock follows the shape of the mountains that are behind it, and therefore it served as an altar to worship the mountains or "Apus."

The enigmatic rock is placed between two buildings called huayranas by the Incas.

This place is known as the Sacred Rock or Stone, leading one to believe that it was an altar to worship the mountains or "Apus," the deity related to water and fertility. The Incas understood that they had to worship their deities, but they also had to show the population that they were intermediaries between those deities and the people. For this reason they adopted the use of geometric and abstract shapes to identify with their gods.

The zigzag for instance, was related to lightening, rain and water and thus to fertility. The pyramids and terraces were artificial mountains that lifted them up to heaven and connected them with their gods. The set of steps symbol that referred to mother earth or "pachamama" was present in every Inca construction. The curving of the tower or Temple of the Sun indicated the movement of the heavenly body between solstices, which is evident through their solstice windows. The Intihuatana, at the highest point of the city, allowed the Incas to worship the sun and beg for its permanence. The Sacred Rock did not escape the liturgical purpose of each place in this sacred, magical and spiritual city. In this sense, the Sacred Rock does not only reproduce the shape of the mountain behind it, but becomes an altar for worshiping and probably a place for sacrifices, and is one more part of the complex Andean ritual system.

A visitor meditates before the Urubamba River canyon, in one of the buildings of the eastern urban sector. In this zone, the architectural design is of lesser quality and uses small cobblestones joined together with mud mortar. It is possible to see the ability of the Incas to make use of the rocks of the mountain as foundations for the buildings by following its shape.

Group of enclosures built next to the Usnu, in the northern sector of the east side of Machu Picchu. There are a series of passages and narrow streets connecting the buildings with each other, which can be seen to be of a lesser quality.

Vizcacha (Lagidium peruanum), Andean rodent, prowling about the urban zone.

HIGH GROUP

Also known as the Northern Quarter, it is the highest set of buildings of the eastern urban sector (at the other side of the Main Square). It is separated from the Sacred Rock by a half pyramid called "Usnu" and the east section of the quarter is next to the terraces that support it over the Urubamba River canyon.

One of the wide enclosures of the High Group. Some investigators suggest that these buildings served as classrooms for students.

General view of the Eastern Urban Sector.
From left to right, the High Group, the Building of the Three Portals and the Industrial Quarter.

BUILDING OF THE THREE PORTALS

It is really a group of enclosures with three identical portals which can be seen inside the grouping. It is located in the center of the eastern urban sector, between the High Group and the so-called Industrial Quarter.

It can be reached from the Main Square through a long stairway that climbs over two large terraces that separate it from the square. Bingham found a series of "quipus" in this place. This is why he called it the Intellectuals Quarter.

Something about this area that attracts attention is that it is composed of three identical buildings, with the same number of rooms, of the same measurements and arrangement, and three identical portals that give the group its name.

Building of the Three Portals.

The Intellectuals Quarter, according to Bingham. The stone block resting lying in the room was probably going to be modified or carved to make an altar.

Inside passage of the group of rooms of the Building of the Three Portals.

Orchid of the zone (Prosthechea vespa).

Spectacled bear
(Tremarctos ornatus).

Ample room at
the east side of
the mountain
with
Putucusi in front.

Interesting building with a double row of trapezoidal niches at the Industrial Quarter.

Beautiful trapezoidal door in one of the rooms. There are no stairways to connect with the back buildings, so there probably used to be one made of wood.

Room or Palace of the Mortars.

These mortar-shaped carved rocks are for some, "eyes" to observe the sky.

INDUSTRIAL QUARTER

Hiram Bingham named this set of buildings the Industrial Quarter. It is located between the Building of the Three Portals and the Prison Group or Temple of the Condor. The discoverer of Machu Picchu named it so because he supposed that the Machu Picchu craftsmen lived and worked there. He arrived at this conclusion because there are two circular rocks protruding from the floor that have been carved as mortars. Nevertheless it is easy to observe that these rocks were not used as mortars since they do not show any wear. On the contrary, they look finely and homogenously polished. They could have been elements used for some religious rite for some kind of payment with "chicha" (corn beer) or blood. Notice that if they are filled with water or any other liquid, the reflection of the sun, the moon or some stars can be seen in them.

Small altar north of this quarter.

Notice the perfection of the joints of the stone blocks in this room of the Industrial Quarter.

Temple of the Condor or Prison Group. In the foreground on the floor, the representation of the head of the bird. On top, the shape of the rock suggests the spread wings.

TEMPLE OF THE CONDOR

It is located at the southern side of the east urban sector of Machu Picchu and because of its subterranean dungeons, it is also called the Prison Group. The name Temple of the Condor comes from the shape of a condor with spread wings with a clearly carved head on a rock on the floor and niches that would have served as cells, over the wings.

These jails show three types of confinements. The first type were subterranean ones which were dark and humid dungeons. Some believe prisoners were tortured there using poisonous and savage animals, such as spiders and serpents.

Row of niches the size of a person where the prisoners were walled in, with only a hole to breathe and be fed.

One of the
subterranean cells.

Lateral stairway
entering the temple.

These niches located over one of the wings could have served to immobilize the prisoners, introducing their hands through the holes at the sides. Nevertheless, some maintain that they were altars to worship mummies.

The second type were on top of the building and consisted of a row of nine niches parallel to the Main Square. It is believed that the prisoner was placed there and then the niche was covered with blocks of adobe or stone, leaving only an opening for him to breath and be fed. The third one is located over the wings of what would be the representation of the condor. There, the niches show holes on the lateral walls where, it is said, the prisoner's hands would be placed and tied up by the wrists. However, others suggest that these niches did not form part of the prison, but were altars where the mummies were placed during the rites related to the condor, one of the Inca deities.

Detail of the holes where the prisoner's hands were placed.

View from the left wing. The tunnel leading to the subterranean cells can be seen in the middle.

The Temple of the Condor in the foreground. Further up are the terraces of the agricultural sector and the Guardian Houses. The Caretaker's hut is on the top.

Huayna Picchu

Huayna Picchu means young peak and it is the mountain located north of the Inca city, but above all, it is the icon by which Machu Picchu is known. Its highest point is at 2700 masl and offers splendid views of Machu Picchu and the adjoining mountains. Climbing it is a bit dangerous, but it can be done.

Huayna Picchu was used by the Incas to build some complexes like the impressive Temple of the Moon, located in the back of the mountain. The Incas also built a series of small terraces at the top, as well as some rooms, apart from an altar that is now in very poor condition. These buildings may have been part of an observatory, and maybe also served as a watching point, since absolutely all of Machu Picchu, Inti Punku and the roads leading to the city can be observed from there.

At the top of Huayna Picchu.

Dangerous set of steps leading to the top of Huayna Picchu.

Opposite page: Machu Picchu from Huayna Picchu. Some see the shape of a condor with spread wings.

Narrow road on Huayna Picchu. The Inca city can be seen to the right, as also the summit of the Machu Picchu mountain.

The beautiful Temple of the Moon, inside a cavern adapted by the Incas.

TEMPLE OF THE MOON

This is an archeological group located at the back of Huayna Picchu mountain (northern side). It is one of the most beautiful Inca constructions built inside a cavern and to which stone blocks have been added fitting perfectly with each other not leaving even a millimeter between them.

It has fine-looking niches of the typical Inca style, and there is a rock at the front, carved in the shape of an altar, leading to believe that this place was used for sacrifices. The whole complex is positioned at different levels, with the lower one having the nicer finish, being located where the temple and its altar are.

Rooms built on top and under the rocks, of a lesser finish but impressive.

Strange rectangular construction, with trapezoidal doors and windows on the left wall.

View of the inside of the rectangular room. Notice the door spaces and niches on the right.

Stone stairway joining the various rooms of the architectural complex of the Temple of the Moon.

There are some buildings at the top that seem to have served as housing or small military quarters, of a lesser architectural finish, but strategically located in the mountain.

Trapezoidal Inca door of the complex called Temple of the Moon.

INCA TRAIL

In Quechua, the language of the Incas, roads were called "Capac Ñan" (Royal Roads). The Incas inherited from the Wari, a great culture before them, a vast road network that they later on improved and extended to undertake their expansion enterprise. These roads were also used by the Spanish to move about and defeat the Incas.

Four large stretches of road started from the center of the Tahuantinsuyu, Cusco, and extended everywhere. These four main roads led to the four Suyus, or large regions of the Inca State. However, the two main roads traveled the Tahuantinsuyu from South to North, one through the Andes mountain range and the other along the coastal strip. Between them, there was a net of secondary and minor roads that connected the various towns, communities and agricultural production centers. An estimate made of all Inca roads taking into account the main roads and the secondary ones, fluctuated between 25,000 and 30,000 km.

The roads were constructed using local materials. In the Andes they used stones to set the foundations and in the coast they used gravel. Today these roads exist in different areas of Peru, Ecuador, Bolivia, Chile and Argentina. In every road they built resting places for messengers (chasquis) and soldiers called "tambos."

Opposite page; Tourist trekking the Inca Trail.

Stretch of the Inca road leading to Machu Picchu that was carved on the natural rock forming steps.

Inca road made with cobblestones.

In this way, the Incas kept a fast communication system with a network of messengers who ran in stages carrying the news, coded in the "quipus" or orally transmitted.

It is also known that the Inca, whose habitual residence was in Cusco, liked to eat fresh fish, which was transported from the coast of the present Arequipa through the efficient Inca roads and their fast messengers, "chasquis". The Incas did not use wheels, but in the slanting mountains of the Andes, it would have been very difficult to use wheels.

The Inca roads also entered the rain forest region, for example the road connecting Machu Picchu and Vilcabamba or the one that enters Chachapoyas in the north or the "Gran Pajatén" in the National Park of the Abiseo River, in the nor-eastern department of San Martin. They also crossed and bordered deserts as dry as that of Atacama in Chile or Sechura, north of Peru. To cross the rivers, the Incas built hanging bridges, knitted with vegetable fibers and renewed them every year, since rain damaged them. And to cross the mountains, the roads reached passes that often were located at more than 4,000 masl.

INCA TRAIL

Entrance to the Inca Trail at kilometer 82.

Before discovering Machu Picchu, Bingham and his expedition found some Inca stretches of road. However, it was not until 1915 after reaching Vilcabamba that Bingham realized the importance of these roads and made a public announcement of their existence. However, these roads had always been used by the local inhabitants and even other modern asphalt roads were built over them (a clear example of this can be seen in the Tambo Colorado complex, near Pisco, 220 km south of Lima).

In 1941 the Wenner-Gren Foundation expedition, headed by the Hungarian Paul Fejos, arrived to study the Inca roads of the region and one of their great findings was the spectacular Wiñay Wayna complex.

The trekking route of the Inca Trail to Machu Picchu may begin, taking as a reference the distance in kilometers of the railway tracks from Cusco to Machu Picchu, at km 78 (Chilca station), at 82 (Piscachuco), at 88 (Qorihuayrachina) or at km 104. The latter one takes two days to cover while the others take four days.

Starting at Chilca and crossing the bridge over the Urubamba River, there are nine kilometers of easy walk until one reaches the Llactapata or Patallacta archaeological complex. Entering through Piscacucho, the walk is similar as that from Chilca, almost flat. Note

that Chilca is slightly higher than Patallacta (see map on page 126). The snow capped peak of the Veronica Mountain whose name in Quechua is Huacayhuilca (5750m), can be seen from the road.

Porters of the Inca Trail weigh the baggage they will carry on their backs. They are only allowed to carry a maximum of 25 kilos per person.

Personnel from the agencies that guide the tourists prepare the equipment to be used on the Inca Trail.

Bridge over the Urubamba River and Inca Trail entrance.

The journey starting at kilometer 88, Qorihuayrachina, climbs eastwards, with the Q'ente ruines on the opposite side. Climbing continues until one reaches the Cusichaca River, which is crossed near the Patallacta or Llactapata complex.

The plant life along the Inca Trail is abundant.

Travelling light, water at hand and a walking-stick to start the journey.

The Veronica snow capped mountain illuminated by the last sunrays of the afternoon.

LLACTAPATA (2650 M)

Also known as Patallacta, its name translated from Quechua would mean "town in a place". It is a vast archaeological complex of what must have been a fortified city located on the Cusichaca River. This flows into the Urubamba River, not very far from there.

The large extent of terracing gave the area stability and created flat terraces for agriculture. The large number of houses, squares, passages and constructions, lead to the belief that this place did not only house residents but was used for the administration of agricultural production.

The historian from Cusco, Victor Angles, analysed this complex structure and distribution. He stated that "the eastern strip of Llactapata is the largest one; it is the lowest riverside sector, with flat and horizontal fields destined for agricul-

Series of buildings at Llactapata. A pattern is reapeted: A central square surrounded by buildings with doors facing the square and windows to the east.

ture and possibly also to locate adobe houses for the people…" We can ascertain that the Incas used stone buildings for the nobility and religious authori-

ties. The people lived in modest dwellings made of mud, cane and other inexpensive materials that have left no visible traces.

General view of the Llactapata complex. Notice the fortified wall next to River Cusichaca.
A round tower of appealing design can be seen at the right end.

The rooms located at the east side are quite long, with several trapezoidal windows and niches.

Circular tower at Llactapata, called Pulpituyuj, It is located at the east end of the complex, in the lower level, close to the wall next to the Cusichaca River. It was built over a great rock and it may have been a ceremonial center, jail or a sacrificial altar.

This building has niches similar to those of the Temple of the Condor in Machu Picchu, with the perforations on the sides.

Pullpituyuj tower, seen from one of the windows of the top part of the complex. Its name is not original, since it comes from the fusion of the Spanish word "púlpito" (pulpit) and the Quechua ending "yuj". Together meaning place with a pulpit.

Huayllabamba, meaning meadow, is the largest and last community in the Inca Trail to Machu Picchu. It is located at 3060 masl.

Warmiwañusca means dead woman and there is an "apacheta" or heap of stones that Andean hikers usually place at the highest points of roads in the belief that they must make payments to the mother earth.

Small stretch of road with a different microclimate: very hot and humid, lots of vegetation and water fountains.

WARMIWAÑUSCA

The Warmiwañusca pass, the highest on the road with an altitude of 4215m, is reached on the second day of trekking of a four-day journey.

The second day starts at this point from where more than 1000 meters will be climbed.

Ascending road to the Warmiwañusca Pass, it is the hardest part of the entire Inca Trail.

Ascension to the Warmiwañusca Pass, very close to the goal.

Warmiwañusca Pass. This point of the trail is quite high and cold and one can feel the lack of oxygen. It is recommended not to remain there for very long.

Sunrise at
Pacaymayu Camp.

Warmiwañusca Pass.

RUNCURACAY

This is not the original name of the archaeological complex, this name was given to it in 1915 by the workers that were cleaning the place following Hiram Bingham's orders. Its name means oval shaped fortification and its purpose, as can be seen, was to serve as a "tambo" or a place of rest. Facing the fortification is the Pacaymayu ravine and its strategic position offers a spectacular view of the zone.

Down right:
Occidental side of the Warmiwañusca Pass. The long Inca Trail can be seen going down to the Pacaymayu (hidden river) valley and then going up to Runcuracay, the second Pass. Camp is usually set up down the valley on the second night.

Group of hikers
and their porters set up camp for lunch after going through the Warmiwañusca Pass.

Semicircular wall of the fortified Runcuracay construction. The Inca road can be seen at the top going up to the second pass of the journey.

General view of the fortified Runcuracay complex and the ravine of the Pacaymayu valley.

Arrival at the Runcuracay complex. 3760 meters.

Beautiful wild flower of the area.

The landscape gets greener, with more life and water as the road starts going down to Sayacmarca. In the photograph, the Green Lake or Q'omercocha.

Runcuracay Pass, located at 3998 meters.

Occidental side of the Runcuracay Pass. Descent and the easiest part of the Inca Trail starts.

General view of the Sayacmarca archaeological complex, on the Inca road to Machu Picchu. Notice the restricted entrance to the citadel through the long and narrow stairway.

SAYACMARCA

This name means inaccessible town and it was given to the place by Paul Fejos expedition in 1941. He did not accept the name that Bingham had given it in 1915 when he was doing investigation work in the area. Bingham had named it Cedrobamba, because he found a small wood of cedar trees in the area (the word bamba is the Spanish vulgarization of the Quechua word pampa, meaning place).

This complex is located at 3600 meters on top of a steep mountain (hence the name). Its buildings were adapted to the difficult shapes of the mountain, from where the whole Aobamba Valley can be seen.

The complex makes an impact because there are so many rooms, squares, water channels, and liturgical fountains that have been built on such a small space and so close to the precipice. The scholars believe that it was a sacred center related to the observation of the sky, intelligently protected and difficult to reach.

In the foreground, the perimeter Sayacmarca wall. Down the ravine over a half-pyramid, the building called Qonchamarca, whose ritual characteristics can be seen.

Semicircular room on the top part of the complex. Its characteristics are those of a religious or worshiping center. The water channel on the left comes from up the mountain, in the background.

Orchid on the Inca Trail (Cranichis ciliata).

The architectural characteristics of the complex have a lesser quality finish. However, the arrangement of buildings on the small landing section of the mountain is impressive.

Bend in the Inca Trail offering a beautiful view of the mountain range.

A twenty meter long tunnel made by the Incas. Steps have been carved on the floor and the walls have been polished.

Part of the Inca Trail joining Sayacmarca with Phuyupatamarca.

PHUYUPATAMARCA

Bingham had discovered and explored these ruins in 1915 and called them Qorihuayrachina. At km 88 of the Machu Picchu railway track there is another archaeological site with the same name. However, it was Paul Fejos who named the place Phuyupatamarca, meaning place, town or city above the clouds. Whoever has been there can verify that the name fits exactly,

because at night the clouds come down to the ravines and the archaeological complex rises over them. At sunrise, the clouds go up due to the heating of the environment.

The complex is fine looking, although the architectural style, called "pirca", is simple. The terraces that hold the complex are symmetrical and keep to the shape of the mountain. Stairways have been built to connect the four groups of buildings with each other and with the house on top.

Phuyupatamarca complex, built over terraces that follow the sinuosity of the mountain.

The respect the Incas had for natural shapes, imitating them the best they could, can be seen by looking at these buildings. The spectacular Intipata archaeological compound can be seen on the top part of the photo.

The highest part of Phuyupatamarca, 3680 m. There is a good camping place here.

There are six water fountains of liturgical character next to one of the sides of the terraces. The semi-circular tower that gives the place a military look, also stands out.

General view from the Inca Trail of the spectacular archaeological ruins of Intipata, located at 2800 meters.

INTIPATA

This complex, located very near Machu Picchu, was discovered by the expedition headed by Paul Fejos in 1941 and was given a name that means place of the sun. Maybe the name is justified by the fact that Intipata looks to the east and the first sunrays of dawn illuminate it completely with a special kind of light.

The place is a vast complex of terraces (48) over which a series of enclosures have been built as well as four stairways that permit walking all around it.

Windows, niches and trapezoidal doors are the characteristics of the rooms of the complex. The enclosures follow the shape of the mountain.

Below Intipata, the Wiñay Wayna complex is located half way down the mountain. A stretch of the Inca Trail that goes up from km 104 of the railway track, can be seen in front of it. Phuyupatamarca with which there was visual contact, is on the upper side, to the right.

Interior of an apparently two- storied room. The stone in the shape of a mortar in the foreground seems peculiar.

Steep stairways that go through the 48 terraces of the complex. The Urubamba River flows in the bottom of the canyon.

Water channel coming down from the top alongside the steps and the terraces. Intipata means place of the sun and the beautiful sunlight of dawn justifies the name the expedition of Paul Fejos chose for it in 1941. The original name of the complex is unknown.

Wiñay Wayna or Forever Young orchid (Epidendrum secundum), that gave its name to this extraordinary complex.

Internal part of the semicircular tower located on the upper zone. The windows and doors of the building face the Urubamba River canyon.

In the foreground, the ceremonial fountains. Downhill is the lower complex in Wiñay Wayna. A bit further, the Urubamba River. In the middle of the mountain facing the complex, the Inca Trail that borders it can be seen.

WIÑAY WAYNA

This impressive archaeological complex was discovered in 1941 by Paul Fejos and studied by him and by the Peruvian archaeologist Julio C. Tello in 1942. The place was named after a very common orchid of the area: Wiñay Wayna (Epidendrum secundum). In English this means "forever young". This plant is abundant in the sanctuary and was very well known by the Incas. So much so that the half Inca, half Spanish chronicler Garcilaso de la Vega, describes it in his "Comentarios Reales" (Royal Comments).

Wiñay Wayna is located at 2630 masl and its cloud forest climate makes it an adequate habitat for numerous flora and fauna species. The complex is located in the middle of the mountain and rests on big

Wiñay Wayna in all its splendor.

series of terraces that, as in Machu Picchu, form an agricultural sector.

The urban sector is formed by a group of rectangular, one and two-storied buildings with trapezoidal windows, niches and doors, streets and passages, stairways, squares and liturgical fountains, all of typical Inca form.

On the top part there is a semicircular construction, with an entrance through a double-jamb door. Apparently, it was an observation and military control point owing to its location and perfect visual control of the surroundings, although some scholars apply a religious character to the building.

At one of its sides, there is a row of ten identical, liturgical fountains going from top to bottom following the slope of the mountain and the arrangement of the terraces. In the same way as Machu Picchu and other Inca locations, these fountains had a ritual purpose related to the worship of water and fertility of the land.

Waterfall at Wiñay Wayna next to the Inca Trail.

Double jamb main entrance to the top part of the complex.

Window of the semicircular tower at the top of Wiñay Wayna.

Small, inside square and two-storied buildings at the lower level. The tower and lateral terraces can be seen on top. All the buildings display the stone spikes that served to hold the roofs.

Our Inca Trail porters pose on arrival at Machu Picchu.

Row of buildings facing east, towards the Urubamba River canyon.

CHOQUEQUIRAU

Contrary to what happened with Machu Picchu, the Choquequirau (gold vein) ruins were known by the inhabitants of nearby communities, as well as by different travelers and adventurers searching for hidden Inca treasures. And also by the Spaniards who after having conquered the Inca estate, dedicated themselves to looting all the Inca temples, palaces and cemeteries looking for gold, and Choquequirau was no exception.

Choquequirau (3033 masl) is located in the department or region of Cusco, but to reach it, one has to go through Abancay, from the town of Cachora. After Cusco fell to the Spaniards, the last Incas, took refuge in Vilcabamba and resisted the military pursuit of the Spanish conquistadors until 1572. Choquequirau was connected to Vilcabamanca through an Inca road and maybe this was one of the last Inca resistance settlements.

There are documented reports that give account of the visits of different people to these ruins, in the XVIII century as well as later on. Among them the following stand out: Eugene de Sartiges and Antonio Raimondi in the XIX century and Hiram Bingham in 1909.

When leaving Cachora to go over to the Choquequirau ruins, it is necessary to travel 30 km on foot through narrow roads going down to the Apurimac River and then up to the ruins.

Opposite page: Choquequirau

Narrow, dry and slippery road on the way down to the Apurimac Canyon.

CHOQUEQUIRAU

Vilcabamba snow-capped mountain range on the way to Choquequirau.

Occidental side of the Apurimac River canyon. Choquequirau can be seen in the background.

Last stretch before reaching the mountain bearing the same name as the ruins: Choquequirau.

Andean Cock of the Rocks (Rupicola Peruviana).

CHOQUEQUIRAU

Lateral entrances to the residence of ancestors' mummies.

High or Hanan sector.

Long room, called callanca, at the High Sector.
It was somewhat narrow to house people; the buildings on the left may have been for storage.

HIGH SECTOR

Choquequirau may be divided in accordance with the location of its buildings and monuments into three large areas: the High or Hanan Sector, the Lower or Hurin sector and the Usnu or Ceremonial Platform.

The High Sector is composed of the group of buildings, squares, water fountains, passages and stairways that are located north of the complex. This is a predominantly liturgical sector, with a ceremonial square and a group of enclosures and a ceremonial water fountain in front. These enclosures seem to have served as residence for mummies and all the complexes may have been used for fertility rites or water worshiping. The water coming out of this fountain runs

through several channels to other points in the complex.

There are some rectangular quarters in the lower part of this sector with doors facing east. For some investigators, these may have been military quarters. However, there is no consensus since others maintain that they were ceremonial rooms. What is true is that buildings of these characteristics are known as "callancas" in Quechua.

Building at the northern end of the complex that may have been used as residence and place of worship of mummies.

CHOQUEQUIRAU

Water channel coming from this building at the High Sector.

Water channel that starts at the High Sector and goes down to the Lower Sector. The Usnu or Ceremonial Platform rests on top of the mountain in front.

Narrow rooms of the High Sector.

Terraces in the High Sector with the Usnu facing them.

Small terraces one after the other. They have a wall at both sides with a small trapezoidal niche, which leads one to believe they had a liturgical purpose.

Pentagonal square at the Lower or Hurin Sector, seen from the Usnu.

LOW SECTOR

This is the area one meets when entering the complex from the lateral terraces, following the present road that is not the original Inca road. The pentagonal square comes first in this sector. This plaza is surrounded by buildings on three of its sides, leaving the eastern side open, where the entrance terraces are located. The so-called Triumphal Wall and the Usnu are on the southeastern side.

There is a rectangular building of the callanca type with four doors, west of the square. The construction of this callanca is peculiar, since the doors are alternated with niches the size of a door so as to allow for a person to stand in it, with a small niche on the upper part. It has the same type of trapezoidal niches on the interior walls and some stone security gadgets that offer more mystery than light as to the purpose of this construction. However, it can be said, given its location on the square, that it was used for ceremonial rather than military purposes, or for jails, housing or workshops. In this sense, the idea some have that it was used to house the virgins that were to be sacrificed during fertility rites, is not outlandish.

North of the square there is a two-storied building connected to two other very similar ones through narrow passages. Archeologists agree in pointing out that these buildings form a group that could be considered a palace of fine architectural finish. There are niches in the second level and a lateral access door precisely for the upper level, while the two doors facing the square were used for the first floor only.

Next to this palace there is another construction similar to the callanca that is rectangular and long. This callanca has six doors facing east and many large niches on the inside walls. Behind this area, there is a group of buildings of different characteristics that could have served as a service area for the palace and the callancas.

At the opposite side of the street there are three constructions. One of them has a semicircular wall, suggesting they were three houses connected by a water channel that comes down from the top part of the Choquequirau complex and leads to a liturgical fountain located in the most western room of these three houses. Even though the purpose of these buildings is not known, they probably were connected with land fertility rites where water played a divine role.

Callanca seen from the septentrional side. The pentagonal square is next to it and in the back over the Triumphal Wall is the Usnu.

Façade of the callanca. Notice the niches in between the four entrance doors.

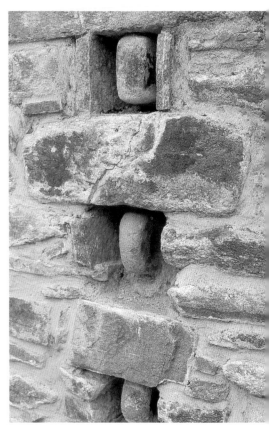

Interior of the callanca. The mysterious niches on the inside walls arrest the attention of scholars, who up to now have not been able to explain their purpose.

Detail of the safety mechanism present on each niche of this room.

View of one of the three royal buildings. Notice the beautiful niche with window located between both doors. However, to have used concrete beams for reconstructing some doors, as can be seen from the door at the right, is reprehensible.

Facade of the first of three similar buildings of a palace complex. The niches of the second level can be seen as well as one of the lateral doors of the top floor. The door to the right connects with a passage connecting the three buildings.

Orchid
Sobralia
dichotoma.

Entrance door to the passage connecting the three similar buildings, probably houses of the nobility.

View from the inside out of the passage connecting the royal buildings.

Royal palace at Choquequirau, a beautiful architectural piece.

Interior of the callanca of the six doors. It is quite a lot wider than the one located on the square and its wall niches are smaller. The niches on the right wall are of the window type. The protruding cylindrical stone supports are too low to have served to hold the roof. They must have served another purpose.

Inca palace interior. Notice the niches of the first and second floor.

Group of three houses located southwest of the square. To the right is the water channel that comes down from the High Sector and finally drains into a water fountain located in the last of these three houses. A little further up is the Triumphal Wall and the Usnu rises in the back.

Semicircular wall of one of the enclosures of the southwest sector. The passage leads to the pentagonal square.

Ceremonial water fountain located in the last house of this sector.

Triumphal Wall.

TRIUMPHAL WALL

South of the pentagonal square located at the point where the Usnu slope starts, there is a smaller square with the Triumphal Wall at its southern end. Sartiges named it this way in 1850 (*mur triomphal*). The archeologists and investigators of this place prefer to call it *wall of the offerings to the ancestors*, because the ceremonial Usnu located on the back hill as a kind of anteroom, forms part of it.

This Triumphal Wall consists of a great wall with four niches placed at different levels and an access door to the Usnu, all of them of trapezoidal shape. It is undoubtedly, a beautiful example of Inca architecture, very well made and of typical liturgical and ceremonial quality.

Two of the niches seem to be doors and the other two, windows. The construction was high, from what can be observed, probably two-storied as is very usual in Choquequirau. On the opposite side from the entrance door, there is a small room of low walls facing the mountain side. This room has a small niche on its back wall, which leads to the belief that its purpose was related to the ceremonial activities of the square.

Entrance to one to the niches of the Triumphal Wall.

CHOQUEQUIRAU

Entrance door to the ceremonial Usnu.

Inside part of the Triumphal Wall. The niches are to the left and to the right is the entrance from the square.

The mountain rising in the background corresponds to the ceremonial Usnu. In front of it is theTriumphal Wall. In the foreground, the water channel coming down from the High Sector.

CHOQUEQUIRAU

Back section of the entrance to the Usnu. The pentagonal square and its buildings can be seen in front and to the left the water channel coming down from the High Sector, and to the right are the terraces of the present entrance to the complex.

One of the terraces of Choquequirau.

Outside steps that connect the terraces on the east side of the complex.

Ceremonial Usnu at Choquequirau, seen from the High Sector or Hanan. Within Inca architecture, this kind of half pyramid was used for religious or military ceremonies.

The Choquequirau Usnu has a small perimeter wall.

Dawn at Choquequirau.

CHOQUEQUIRAU

N

Lake Salcantaycocha

Tucarhuay
Snow Capped Mountain

Qoriwayrachina
Snow Capped Mountain

Padreyoc
Snow Capped Mountain

Q. Chalan

Amparay Mountain

Blanco River

Q. Paccha

Yanajaja Mountain

Soray Mountain

Q. Yanalaja

Q. Nihuabamba

Chaupiloma Mountain

Marcani Mountain

Apurímac River

Q. Pabellucl

Comas River

San Cristobal Mountain

Apurimac River

to C.isco

Curahuasi

REGION OF CUSCO

REGION OF APURIMAC

Mountain Pass Choquequirau
4,080m

Choquequirau
3,033m

Q. Cotacoca

Marampampa
3,000m

Santa Rosa
2,100m

Rosalina Riverside

Apurímac River

Capuliyoc
2,800m

Tabinquillay Mountain

Marancarayoc Mountain

Sayhuite
3,500m

Incahuasi Mountain

Cachora
2,875m

Tambobamba River

Cusilluyoc Mountain

Q. Suchuna

Suchunapata Mountain

Huanipaca

Jastajasa Mountain

Jayune Mountain

Ampay
Snow Capped Mountain

NATIONAL SANTUARY AMPAY

ABANCAY
2,378m

to Nasca

to Ayacucho

KILOMETERS
0   1   2

Cartografía digital: Grupo Geo Graphos

Path to Choquequirau
Departament capital
District capital
Town
Highway
Unpaved road
Bridge
Camp site
Archaeological site
Protected area
Mountain pass

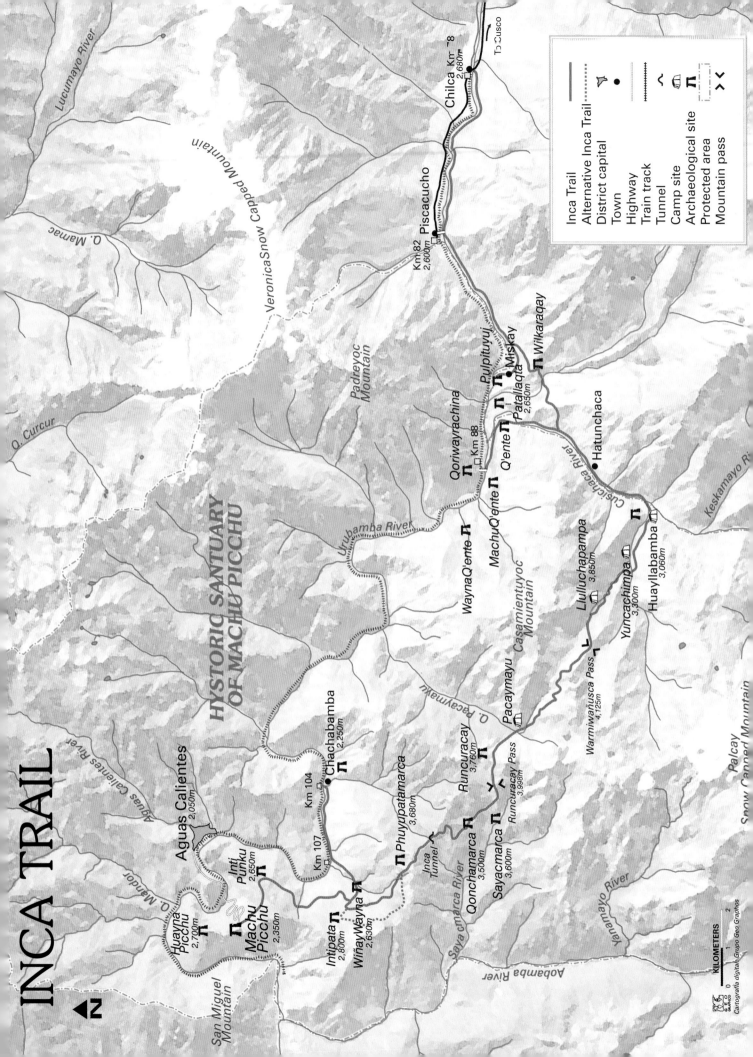

TRAIN TO MACHU PICCHU

Above: The train to Machu Picchu leaves Cusco at dawn. **Below:** Its route follows the Urubamba River.

INDEX